SPORTS ALL-ST★RS

AARON JUDGE

Jon M. Fishman

Lerner Publications ◆ Minneapolis

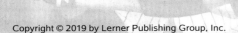

Lerner Publications Company
A division of Lerner Publishing Group, Inc.
241 First Avenue North
Minneapolis, MN 55401 USA

For reading levels and more information, look up this title at www.lernerbooks.com.

Main body text set in Albany Std 15/22. Typeface provided by Agfa.

Library of Congress Cataloging-in-Publication Data

Names: Fishman, Jon M., author.
Title: Aaron Judge / Jon M. Fishman.
Description: Minneapolis : Lerner Publications, 2019. | Series: Sports all-stars |
    Includes bibliographical references and index. | Audience: Age 7–11. | Audience:
    Grade 4 to 6.
Identifiers: LCCN 2017061534 (print) | LCCN 2017060528
    (ebook) | ISBN 9781541524644 (eb pdf) | ISBN 9781541524569 (lb : alk. paper) |
    ISBN 9781541528024 (pb : alk. paper)
Subjects: LCSH: Judge, Aaron, 1992—Juvenile literature. | New York Yankees
    (Baseball team)—Juvenile literature. | Baseball players—United States—Juvenile
    literature.
Classification: LCC GV865.J83 (print) | LCC GV865.J83 F57 2019 (ebook) | DDC
    796.357092 [B]—dc23

LC record available at https://lccn.loc.gov/2017061534

Manufactured in the United States of America
1-44532-34782-5/1/2018

CONTENTS

Aaron Judge hits a home run at Marlins Park in Miami, Florida, in 2017.

Crack! New York Yankees outfielder Aaron Judge crushed the baseball with a mighty swing. It sailed high and deep into the outfield seats at Marlins Park in Miami, Florida. *Crack!* Judge swung again, sending a ball even farther than the previous one. *Crack!* Another swing, another home run!

Judge was taking part in the 2017 Major League Baseball (MLB) **Home Run Derby**. He faced Justin Bour of the Miami Marlins in the first round. Bour had taken his turn first and smacked 22 home runs, the most any player had hit so far.

Judge wasn't worried. He calmly smashed home runs over the outfield wall. One of his homers went 501 feet (153 m), farther than any hit MLB had ever recorded at the derby. Judge hit 23 home runs in all to advance to the next round.

In round 2, Judge took on Los Angeles Dodgers slugger Cody Bellinger. Bellinger hit 12 home runs. Judge stepped to home plate and picked up right where he had stopped in the previous round. Ball after ball rocketed off his bat. He beat Bellinger with ease. Three of Judge's homers sailed farther than 501 feet (153 m).

Bellinger smashes a home run in the 2017 derby.

Next up was Miguel Sano of the Minnesota Twins in the final round. Sano got off to a slow start and ended up with 10 home runs. Judge quickly showed that 10 wouldn't be enough to beat him. He used his smooth, powerful swing to easily hit 11 and win the derby.

Judge had hit some of the fastest and longest home runs baseball fans had ever seen. Put all together in a line, his home runs at the derby would have traveled 3.9 miles (6.3 km). Judge had a great time competing,

Judge poses with his trophy after winning the 2017 Home Run Derby.

and he was thankful for his chance to show the world his power. "I have had wonderful people help me out through the years," he said. "And I can't thank them enough for where I'm at right now."

Judge weighs 285 pounds (129 kg) and stands 6 feet 7 inches (2 m) tall. That makes him the biggest position player in MLB history.

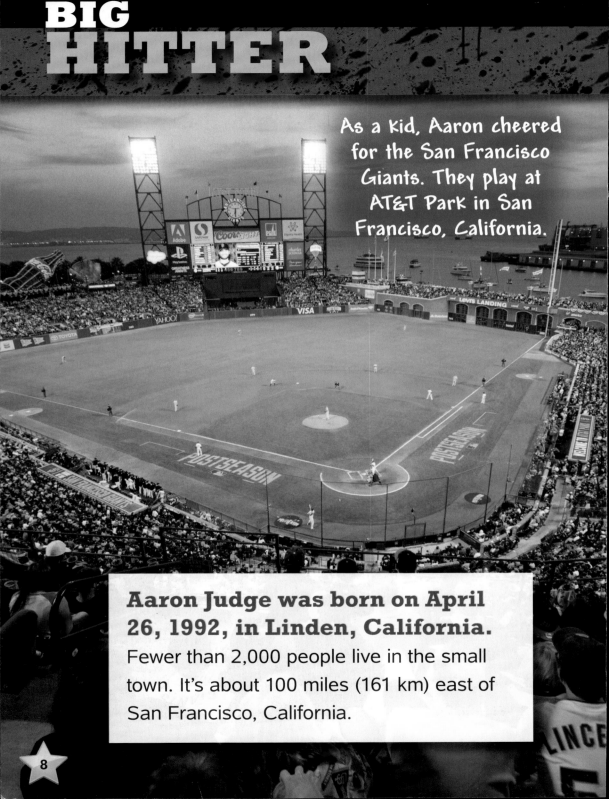

BIG HITTER

As a kid, Aaron cheered for the San Francisco Giants. They play at AT&T Park in San Francisco, California.

Aaron Judge was born on April 26, 1992, in Linden, California. Fewer than 2,000 people live in the small town. It's about 100 miles (161 km) east of San Francisco, California.

On April 27, Wayne and Patty Judge adopted Aaron. They are the only parents he has ever known. In elementary school, Aaron noticed that he didn't look much like his parents. He asked them about it. "They just told me I was adopted, and I said, 'OK, can I go outside and play?'"

Aaron spent a lot of time outside playing sports. He usually stood out as the biggest player on the field. He hit the ball so hard in **T-ball** that players on the other team were scared to face him. They often turned their backs toward home plate to protect themselves when Aaron was at bat.

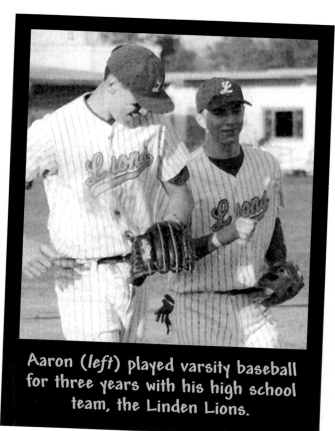

Aaron (*left*) played varsity baseball for three years with his high school team, the Linden Lions.

At Linden High School, Aaron led the **varsity** basketball team and starred as a **wide receiver** for the football team. On the baseball field, he was the team's best hitter *and* pitcher. MLB **scouts** noticed Aaron's size and skills. The Oakland A's chose him in the 31st round of the 2010 MLB **draft**.

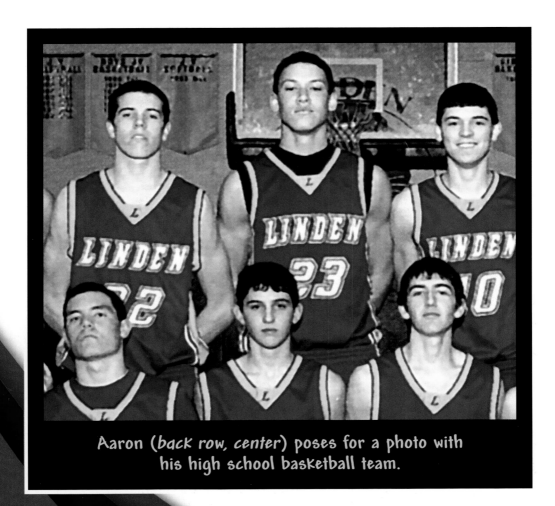

Aaron (back row, center) poses for a photo with his high school basketball team.

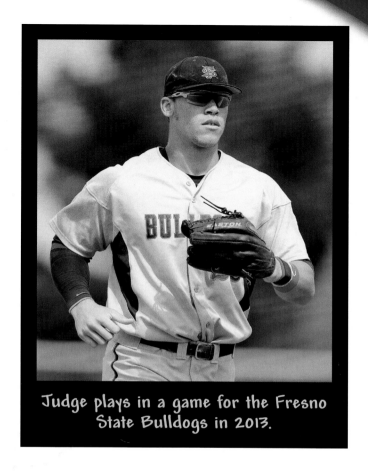

Judge plays in a game for the Fresno State Bulldogs in 2013.

Judge decided that he wasn't ready to play **pro** baseball. "I was set on getting my education," he said. "It was cool and exciting that the A's picked me, but my mind was set." Instead, Judge attended California State University, Fresno (Fresno State).

Judge improved as a baseball player in three seasons at Fresno State. In 2013, he led the team in home runs. He finally felt ready for a pro baseball career. The Yankees chose him in the first round of the 2013 MLB draft.

Judge waits for the pitch in a game in 2017.

Like most MLB players, Judge began his pro career in the **minor leagues**. He spent the next several seasons playing for minor-league teams such as the Charleston RiverDogs and the Trenton Thunder. These teams help young players prepare to play for the Yankees. In 2016, Judge played for the Yankees for the first time. He had a disappointing .179 **batting average** in 27 games. But in 2017, Judge got a chance to play for the Yankees full-time. He quickly became a team leader and one of baseball's most popular stars.

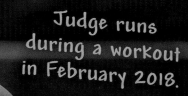

Judge runs during a workout in February 2018.

All MLB players work hard to reach baseball's top level. The game's biggest superstars never stop trying to get better. "There's always room to improve," Judge said. "That motivates me to get a little better every day."

Judge is one of the strongest players in MLB history. He doesn't need to spend much time improving his strength. Instead, he spends most of his gym time in other ways, such as making his body **flexible**. He uses stretchy bands for some workouts. The bands help Judge stretch his muscles as he exercises. Using bands also helps avoid injuries caused by lifting heavy weights.

Judge does plenty of **cardio** workouts to strengthen his heart and lungs. That means running—and jumping. By adding jumps to his workouts, Judge exercises his heart, lungs, and leg muscles at the same time. Jumping also adds fun to a workout. He may set up a row of huge tires and then jump from one to the next.

Judge is strong enough to hit baseballs harder than almost any other player. MLB records the speed of the baseball after a player makes contact with it. In 2017, Judge hit four of the top five fastest balls in the league.

Judge stretches his legs before a 2017 game.

Two more forms of exercise keep Judge in shape mentally and physically—yoga and Pilates. Yoga includes holding certain poses and breathing carefully. The poses stretch and strengthen muscles. Yoga also calms the mind and improves mental focus. Pilates is similar to yoga. During a Pilates workout, people might use equipment such as bars, balls, and stretchy bands in their movements.

Judge stretches
before a game against
the New York Mets.

Of course, Judge still lifts weights to maintain his massive strength. He's also careful about the food he eats. Yankees players have access to plenty of healthful options in the locker room, including fruits, vegetables, and fish. Judge does have at least one less healthful favorite: bubble gum. He always chews two pieces of bubble gum during games. If he gets a hit, he keeps chewing. If he doesn't get a hit, he spits out the gum and gets two new pieces.

Judge chews bubble gum during a 2017 game against the Toronto Blue Jays.

HERO

Judge smiles as he runs toward home plate in a 2017 game.

Yankees fans fell in love with Judge right away. He enjoys being on the field, and his big smile is a common sight at Yankee Stadium. He's confident, but he doesn't like to brag. And, of course, the fans love to watch him smash huge home runs.

To honor Judge, fans began showing up to Yankee Stadium in the robes legal judges wear. Before long, the team provided fans with a special place to sit called the Judge's Chambers. These seats in right field provide an up-close view of Judge in action. On August 31, 2017, a special guest sat in the Judge's Chambers: US Supreme

Judge fans cheer from the Judge's Chambers at Yankee Stadium.

Court justice Sonia Sotomayor. She grew up in New York and has always been a Yankees fan.

Judge fans make themselves known in other ways too. In October 2017, MLB announced that they had sold more Judge jerseys that season than they had sold for any other player. He became just the second **rookie** in MLB history to lead the league in jersey sales. In November, Judge even received 10 votes to become the next mayor of New York City!

Sonia Sotomayor just loves the Yankees!

Judge's Gear

Baseball fans think Aaron Judge is special, and some of them are willing to pay a lot of money to show how they feel. In July 2017, a fan paid $14,000 to buy a baseball card that Judge had signed. A fan bought the jersey Judge was wearing when he hit his first **grand slam** for more than $45,000.

That was just the beginning of the spending spree on Judge gear. Also in July, a fan spent more than $157,000 at an auction for the jersey Judge wore during his first **MLB** game. That price set a record for the most expensive jersey sale in the past 15 years.

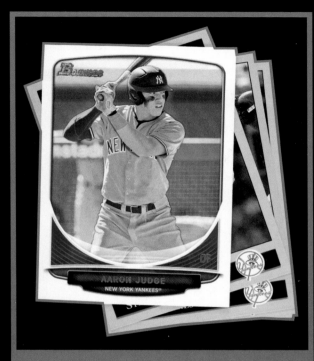

An Aaron Judge baseball card from his rookie season

Judge signs baseballs for fans before a 2016 game.

Judge's popularity has let him have some fun experiences. In May 2017, he appeared in a video that aired on *The Tonight Show Starring Jimmy Fallon*. Wearing glasses as a disguise, Judge asked people funny questions about himself. "I was nervous the whole time," he said.

Judge (*center*) and two of his teammates attend a Brooklyn Nets basketball game in Brooklyn, New York.

Judge runs the bases after hitting his first home run in MLB.

Judge's first MLB at bat came on August 13, 2016. He smashed a long home run that gave fans at Yankee Stadium a thrilling first impression of the team's new star. But he hit just three home runs the rest of the season.

Judge waits for a pitch during the 2017 All-Star Game.

In 2017, Judge hit 10 home runs in April. He had 30 homers before he played in the All-Star Game in the middle of the season. Then he wowed fans around the world by winning the Home Run Derby.

By September 25, Judge had hit an incredible 48 home runs. That meant he was one homer short of tying the all-time season record for a rookie. He smashed two home runs against the Kansas City Royals to set a new record.

By July 2017, Judge had already set the Yankees' record for most home runs by a rookie. Joe DiMaggio had held the previous record for more than 80 years. He hit 29 homers in 1936.

Judge celebrates his 50th home run of the 2017 season with teammate Ronald Torreyes.

Judge poses for photos holding his
Rookie of the Year award.

Judge ended his first season with 52 home runs.
He was the obvious choice to win the American
League Rookie of the Year award. It was an
incredible, record-setting year for the big outfielder.
Yet with Judge's strength, skill, and desire to improve,
his best seasons may be in his future.

All-Star Stats

Rookies often take time to adjust to **MLB**. Hitting 52 home runs in a season is a tough task for any player, especially for a rookie. But Judge blew away most people's expectations in 2017. His 52 blasts rank him ahead of some of baseball's all-time great sluggers.

Most Home Runs in a Season by a Rookie

Player	Season	Home runs
Aaron Judge	2017	52
Mark McGwire	1987	49
Cody Bellinger	2017	39
Frank Robinson	1956	38
Wally Berger	1930	38
Albert Pujols	2001	37
Al Rosen	1950	37
Jose Abreu	2014	36
Mike Piazza	1993	35
Ron Kittle	1983	35
Rudy York	1937	35
Hal Trotsky	1934	35

Source Notes

7   Bryan Hoch, "All(-Star's) Rise! Judge Rules in Derby Debut," MLB, July 11, 2017, http://m.mlb.com/news/article/241596010/aaron-judge-wins-2017-home-run-derby.

9   Bryan Hoch, "Judge: I Wouldn't Be a Yankee without Mom," MLB, May 12, 2017, http://m.mlb.com/news/article/229877552/yankees-aaron-judge-credits-mom-for-success.

11   Randy Miller, "Why Yankees' Aaron Judge Mimicked His Childhood Hero, Giants' Rich Aurilia," *NJ.com*, June 16, 2017, http://www.nj.com/yankees/index.ssf/2017/06/why_yankees_aaron_judge_mimicked_his_childhood_her.html.

13   Bryan Hoch, "Judge: 'I'm Still a Work in Progress,'" MLB, November 10, 2017, http://m.mlb.com/news/article/261253334/yankees-aaron-judge-focused-on-improving.

23   Erik Boland, "Aaron Judge Fools Yankees Fans on 'The Tonight Show' with Jimmy Fallon," *Newsday*, May 16, 2017, https://www.newsday.com/sports/baseball/yankees/aaron-judge-fools-yankees-fans-on-the-tonight-show-with-jimmy-fallon-1.13639373.

Glossary

batting average: a batter's hits per times at bat

cardio: a workout to get the heart pumping and improve blood flow

draft: an event in which teams take turns choosing new players

flexible: able to bend easily

grand slam: a home run hit with a baserunner on every base

Home Run Derby: a yearly MLB event in which players take turns trying to hit home runs

minor leagues: baseball leagues where players train and hope to move up to Major League Baseball

position player: someone who plays one of the eight positions on a baseball field other than pitcher

pro: something done for money that many people do for fun

rookie: a first-year player

scouts: people who judge the skills of athletes

T-ball: baseball for children ages four to six in which the ball is hit from a tee instead of pitched

varsity: the top team at a school

wide receiver: a football player whose main job is to catch passes

Further Information

Aaron Judge
http://m.mlb.com/player/592450/aaron-judge

Braun, Eric. *Super Baseball Infographics*. Minneapolis: Lerner Publications, 2015.

Kelley, K. C. *New York Yankees*. New York: AV2 by Weigl, 2018.

MLB
http://www.mlb.com/mlb/kids

Official Site of the New York Yankees
https://www.mlb.com/yankees

Savage, Jeff. *Baseball Super Stats*. Minneapolis: Lerner Publications, 2018.

Index

Photo Acknowledgments

Image credits: Jim McIsaac/Getty Images, pp. 2 (background), 26; Alex Trautwig/
Major League Baseball/Getty Images, pp. 4–5, 27; Mark Cunningham/Getty Images,
pp. 6, 25; Patrick Farrell/Miami Herald/Tribune News Service/Getty Images, p. 7;
Joseph Sohm/Shutterstock.com, p. 8; Seth Poppel Yearbook Library, pp. 9, 10; Cal
Sport Media/Alamy Stock Photo, p. 11; Josh Lefkowitz/Getty Images, p. 12; Cliff
Welch/Icon Sportswire/Getty Images, p. 13; Mike Ehrmann/Getty Images, p. 15; Paul
Bereswill/Getty Images, pp. 16, 17, 19; Elsa/Getty Images, p. 18; Rich Schultz/Getty
Images, pp. 20, 24; Independent Picture Service, p. 21; Stephen Brashear/Getty
Images, p. 22; James Devaney/WireImage/Getty Images, p. 23.

Cover: Jim McIsaac/Getty Images.